Those Who Trespass

Those Who Trespass

Trespass

by Dan Masterson

The University of Arkansas Press
Fayetteville

The author is grateful to the editors of the following publications in
which the following poems first appeared: *Poetry*: "Safe Distance," *The
New Yorker*: "Calling Home," *The Sewanee Review*: "Yardwork," "A Visit
Home," *The Hudson Review*: "Opening Doors," *The Yale Review*:
"Treehouse," *Poetry Northwest*: "The End of Things," "Pencil," "At the
End of Sleep," "Avalanche," "Night Sky," "Under Cover of Darkness,"
The Massachusetts Review: "Sunday Dinner," *The Denver Quarterly*:
"Rolling the Awning," "Breaking the Seal," *The Memphis State Review*:
"Fitz and the Gandy Dancers," *Esprit*: "Laid Off," "The Woman in the
Corner House," "Feeding the Birds," "Beneath a Mansard Roof."

Sabbatical leaves awarded by Rockland Community College and The
State University of New York enabled the author to complete major
portions of this collection.

LIBRARY OF CONGRESS CATALOGING-IN-PUBLICATION DATA
Masterson, Dan, 1934–
    Those Who Trespass.
    I. Title.
PS3563.A834T5   1985   811'.54   84-28075
ISBN   0-938626-42-6
        0-938626-43-4 (PBK.)

for my father, Stephen, and my mother, Kathleen,
in memory of the early years; and for my daughter,
Martha, and my son, Stephen, in thanks for these,
their beginning years; and for my wife, Janet,
lifeblood for us all

Contents

Five   ***World without End***

ONE

At the Hour of Our Death

Under Cover of Darkness

He's made the flight before,
but never in a wheelchair strapped
back-to-back to the last seat in tourist,
within earshot of a leggy stewardess
complaining of a rough night in Cincinnati.

The secret he's kept in his abdomen
feels like a loaf of bread swallowed whole,
deep in its wraps of flesh and blankets, flexing
its tendrils from hip to groin, sedatives
cooling it down.

He's cold enough to be naked; sure enough
that he's going to explode
that he almost asks for help, but forces
sleep instead. He wakens

To a sinking feeling that takes him aground.
And then a ride flat out
on a canvas litter whose wheels
squeal through the carpeted tunnel,
clearing the way to the terminal with its ceiling
wide as a ballpark. Outdoors they hit
a wind worse than Lake Erie.

Up a rattly old ramp to a hospital van,
complete with a wall of bottles and tubes
and a lanky bag of oxygen draped over its tank.

The trip from La Guardia
reminds him of Verdun, the back roads,
the afternoon of forest patrol in the Argonne,
birds escaping like soot in the sky, safe
from the low cloud of mustard gas sniffing

at his leggings, finding the sweat it needed
to bring him to his knees.

The volunteer at his side looks more
like a street-sweeper, white coveralls baggy
as a clown's, but she knows what he needs
to hear: Deep-breathe when the pain comes;
Exhale it slowly away; Go limp at the bumps:
potholes that could hold their own
in a minefield.

At dusk, they'd settle into the trenches,
scraping hollows in the front wall, and sit
with the war behind them, heads to their knees,
helmets tilted back in case
shell fragments caught them off guard.
The thought makes him shudder,
and he looks at the bulb overhead, wishing
he could cup it in his hands.

She wants to help and assumes
it's a bother. She flicks it off, bringing
the night inside; he takes it in both
eyes, adjusting to it, anxious to see out
the windows of the double back doors.

There are punctual bursts
of arc-lamps, truckers flashing their brights
to pass, billboards lit up
for late commuters.

She is telling him what they will do
at the curb: the unlocking, the lift, the cold
air and nurses waiting to lead him to a stall,
the questions they will ask. She warns him
of the entryway: heaters jutting

from the tiles, an unearthly orange glow
everywhere.

She is calling ahead, giving
estimated arrival time; she spells his last name,
his first, and remembers the PH in Stephen.

The roads curve more in town, just as they did
in Verdun: three weeks in bed,
pampered and groomed. This
will be a shorter stay: The end of the line,
he says to the hand at his face.

The van stops, lurches once
in each direction. The motor runs on, feeding
exhaust through the floorboards. She is up
from her jumpseat, putting a shoulder
to the door.

The blankets are olive drab to his chin.
Strangers take him up and out,
held for a moment
on a rush of cold air
before turning headfirst
into a corridor of orange light.

Opening Doors

He remembered to ease back on the key
before turning to the left. It clicked
open and the tin weatherstripping creaked
as he stepped inside.

Something rushed over him; he went to his knees
and found himself making the sign of the cross:
forehead, breastbone, shoulder, shoulder.
It was as though he'd tried to take a breath
underwater. He stayed put

And pushed the door shut without looking
back. He was staring at the red-ribbed chair
where his father should be, the slippers
under the footstool, a brown cardigan laid
over the armrest for a moment
three weeks ago. In front of him

Was the blanket his mother kept
on the davenport for the naps that gave her
strength for lunch at the kitchen table.

The door swung in at his touch, settling
against the side of the stove. There were dishes
in the drainer, and others left undone
from that last breakfast: two coffee cups
and saucers, a napkin folded at its place,
a plate whose toast was gone.

The door to the back hall was closed,
the skeleton key dangling on its rubberband
from the doorknob. He opened it a crack
and listened; the refrigerator hummed
at full blast. Inside, he saw a half loaf

of bread, some eggs in the door-rack. Three
covered bowls held leftovers from October.

The backdoor key was where it belonged,
on the cuphook near the dustpan. He took
the four steps down and started outside, but
came back in and latched the storm door,
leaving the other ajar. He went downstairs,
flicking the switch with the jolt it always needed.

Near the furnace, beneath the bare bulb,
he took out the list. At the washtubs, he pulled
the lightstring and squatted at the hot-water
tank, thumbing the dust from the dial.
He forced it left and heard the pop.

There were three shirts and a nightgown
on the clothesline that stretched to the fruitcellar.
He dragged his hand across them and turned
the handle of the door he'd helped build.
It needed an upward yank. The high window
was black with paint, but the ceiling switch,
once too high to reach, sent light across the shelves
of canning jars, their rubber rings dried out
in open tins, pans, vases, trays, cardboard boxes
wilting along the seams.

He took the stairs one at a time, almost
starting to count them, but picked up a clothespin
instead. He carried it to the landing and set it
down on the top rim of the milkchute.

Out back, the garage door was locked, the key
out of sight. The lawnmower was wrapped
in oily canvas, the patio chairs stacked
in the corner, the awning rolled, the chipped
white basin still half full of sand for grandchildren.

The red shovel, his own, there on its nail
for fifty years. He lowered the door
and headed for the house, wondering if anyone
saw him, if he should wave.

On the sunporch, he opened the drapes
and attached a timer to the radio. Two others.
One for the floorlamp at the foot of the stairs,
and the last, the guest-room reading light.
New bulbs for both.

His parents' bedroom door was closed.
He wished he could keep it that way. Inside,
the gooseneck lamp was bent low over a saucer
with a spoon upside down in a dried puddle.
A small brown bottle stood close to its cap,
its label toward the wall.
He made the bed and hung his father's robe
on the back of the closet door. The armoire

Was locked. The strongbox was safe
on the bottom shelf, its key in the sock drawer.
There was more than he'd supposed, but he took it
all, filling the suitcase with deeds and stocks,
wills and bonds. He closed
the double doors and locked them.

He sat on the bed and started to give in
to everything around him, but shook it off
and went to his mother's side of the room. Things
were in order. She'd probably stayed awake
that last night, tidying and sorting,
vaguely agreeable, unaware she was walking
through the house for the last time.

He could see the backyard from their window.
It was filling up with snow. He emptied both

drawers of jewelry into a second suitcase and sat
on the bed. He lay back and let it come, all
the summer visits he'd spent there, the talks
with his father, the papers that would take over
at his death: what would become of Mother,
the house, the land.

There was a washcloth next to the sink
and he soaked it. He buried his face in it.
He wrung it out and took a towel
from the linen closet. He left the cloth to dry
on the edge of the tub and dropped the towel
down the laundry chute,
wondering what would become of it.

Pencil

It fits his hand as it had his father's
hand, extra lead stashed inside
beneath a rubber-plug eraser; he'd worn it
clipped in his vest pocket, its arrow,
gold and etched, catching light
as it came toward his desk.

Stolen once from the mantle,
by stick-burglars as we slept, it showed
up at the local precinct, flicking light
from the captain's badge-pocket
as he leaned back in his chair.

After that, it stayed upstairs at night,
weighing lightly down the clean white
handkerchiefs Mother starched and ironed
and stacked in the chifforobe drawer.

The vests are gone, left in plastic bags
with their suits in the Salvation Army shed
at the edge of town, but if the men
who wear them now ever pull the pockets
inside out, they'll find no marks;
he always turned back the lead.

In the strongbox, there are penciled notes,
rough drafts to the bank and hospital:
something about his pension, directions
forbidding the removal of his larynx, and one
which reads in part:

"If I am the first to go, Kathleen,
it is important for you to know,
that we haven't any debts

other than the normal monthly bills.
We have no debts of any kind.
I have not authorized
any delivery of goods or services."

At the End of Sleep

It is always the same: he is far upstate
where the roofs and lawns
are collecting snow.

The sunporch light
is holding his father's profile
to the window. His mother
is turning away
from the oval frame of the front door.

He hurries away unseen,
feeling he has business farther down
the block, but stops at the edge
of the next driveway and goes back,
taking the privet hedge
in one leap, dragging the left foot
as he used to do in the high hurdles
at the cinder track
on the other side of town.

He lands close to the drain vent, its cap
an inch or two above the grass;
he kneels and sees it is the same
perforated lid he scarred on Saturdays
with the handmower.

He taps at the window
next to his father's chair and reads
his lips as he mouths the nickname he used
for a lifetime. He puts his hand
flat to the glass, expecting his father
to do the same, measuring hand
to hand, but his hand is alone, the fingers

feeling the grit that swirls in the air
in that part of the country.

He looks deep into the house. The rooms
are empty. His father's head is cut
from cardboard and stuck to the glass.
A single dab of flour paste, still wet
as milk, begins its run
down the cold clear pane between them.

Yardwork

The fresh drifts slant like poured salt
against the picket fence. Voices,
familiar to the room, suggest
an earlier season:

> There is a man bent to his garden,
> the first warmth come early
> to his back, muscular
> as the earth he kneels in.
>
> Across the lawn, her left hand
> cupped like a vase, a woman
> gathers lilies of the valley, each bell
> ringing to her touch.

And then they are gone. Nothing
but birds at the kitchen window, three
of them perched in twin evergreens,
fluttering snow from the heavy branches.

Rolling the Awning

He used to wrestle it up
the side of the house with his son;
leaning from ladders, hand over hand
they'd go, a rung at a time,
the bulk of canvas collapsing at last
into its storage box for the winter:
that warehouse coffin of a thing
nailed to the clapboards and studs
high against the outside wall.

And then his grandson took his place
while he, cardiac arms overhead, stood
stiff on a patio chair
beginning the roll, until he was left
below, turning the air between us,
the green cracked cloth getting away
from him, the silver bars caging him in
from the sky, the silver bars
naked to the autumn heat come to tease
him toward a season he would never need
an awning for, an awning whose shade
would be given away to strangers
none of us would ever know.

Calling Home

He dials his dead father's house,
where timers go off at noon, at dusk,
at nine, allowing the gooseneck lamp
to come on in the den, the radio
to sift through the kitchen walls
and awaken the neighbor's dog,
who no longer waits at the side door
for scraps.

Six rings—Mother
would have answered by now,
but she's kept in a vest that is tied
to a chair in the rest home he chose
from a list when he was in town.

Twenty rings, and counting:
the pilot light flickers in the stove,
a cobweb undulates
imperceptibly above the sink, the crystal
stemware chimes in its breakfront.

He closes his eyes and listens.
He would like to say something,
but there is nowhere
to begin.

T W O

Sins of Forgiveness

Night Sky

O, Father,
there on the tallest star,
I promised you too much
for my own good. I cannot go
daily to your wife.

I try, instead, to stop by
once a week to wheel her down
the double ramps in time
for lunch, if I'm intact enough
to get beyond my own impending age
which closes in like winter chill
about my legs.

She is in great comfort: fed
well, bathed lovingly, talked to
and watched, given flowers
to arrange and plants to keep
alive. I am never

Her son; sometimes a brother,
a schoolmate whose name
she can't recall, and once,
a month ago, I spent an hour
as her father. She thinks
she is at home, that you
are about to enter every door.

Treehouse

He backs out the nails
but the railings hold fast, ingrown
on the tracks of a ruined oak
rising half dead on the moonlit side
of the lawn.

On a crisscross of scraps and tenpenny nails,
he finds the initials they carved without him
in the glare of a dimestore lantern
long gone from the hook
that gives way at his touch.

He dismantles it all, piece by piece,
sailing each hunk to the foot
of the ladder strapped to the tree.

The roof has worn away;
only a strip of canvas puckers along
its hem of tacks; he takes them
one at a time.

Finished, he climbs down and sits
on the boulder he used to hope
they would miss
if they fell from their sleep.

He looks up at too many branches,
too much sky, and begins
to do what he taught them to do
when they begged for a place
of their own in the leaves.

He collects all the wood
he can hold and goes back up

to rebuild the past: each board
falling into place, its nails returned
without question.

At midnight, he unties the ladder
and lets it slide away to the ground;
he lies flat out, extending his arms
and legs, until he is touching
the trunks of four oaks,
spread-eagle in the middle of the night.

The End of Things

Supper tonight was served by strangers
in a truckstop far from the kitchen sink
where his mother stood watching him back out
over gravel, too close to the oak he scraped
more than once on those late nights they warned
him about. Perhaps he's had enough.

His room is fast becoming a shrine: clean linen,
homework arranged near his books, fresh flowers
at the door, new pajamas folded at the pillow
he should come home to, and the lamp: its limp Christ,
with a 7½ watt candle in His fist, nailed
to the window jamb.

The father wakens in the night and carries a drink
upstairs to disturb the room. He feels the bed,
empty in the half-light. He flicks off the lamp
and studies the shapes of his son's belongings,
hoping to find things missing, but they are there.

The B-29 they built together
holds on to the sky by a thumbtack the size
of a button on a puffcoat, the one his son wore
the last time he saw him slamming out
through the pantry, his answer cut off
by the banging of the door.

He needs another drink, but lies down
instead, his head sinking in
where his son's should be. In what approximates
sleep, he hears a voice behind the bed.
He rouses to speak his name, to coax him back home,
but sunlight comes to wash it all away.

He scatters the homework and curses his wife
and her fastidious shrine. Downstairs
it is the same. No one will look at him. They know
he's been drinking. He leaves them alone
and goes off to his den, to his tall window,
his son behind the mower, the hedge
fencing him in on three sides. But it is only
a tree moving in the snow.

He hears his wife and daughter in the hall,
their quiet voices keeping the walls from falling in.
They shout Goodbye and leave for the day.
He feels better already. He pours himself a drink
and heads for the yard, in search of kindling
felled by the winds that worked all night. He sets
the empty glass at the edge of the woods and goes in.

Loaded to the chin, he comes to the front
of the garage and lays a fire as his son would
have it: twigs tangled like a bird's nest,
sticks forming an open box, and narrow limbs
the size of rake handles to finish it off right
in the middle of the driveway.

Inside for a clean glass, bourbon, and ice.
And then the flame: the first strike does it.
The kitchen match goes white and orange and blue.
But he is gone, back inside,

Upstairs at the window, jamming the storm sash up
as far as it goes. And now it begins. Here come
the pillows and sheets and blanket. A shelf wrenched
from the closet wall. The straightback chair
breaks when it hits the cement. The desk
is too big and takes the windowframe with it:
glass and putty sailing like ice and snow.

The single mattress bounces when it hits. The box
spring cracks once and falls to its side.

And now a wait while the rug is rolled
and lowered by its fringe.

Here, the pajamas unfolding. Homework flying
like kites, books by the dozen flapping
to the ground. The model plane is off its tack,
heading for the fire.

Drawers and their sweaters are on their way,
a closet floor of shoes and boots, shirts, jeans
by the armful, jackets and ties, two stereo speakers,
a double rack of albums, lacrosse sticks
and helmet, bedsides and headboards, a clock
trailing its cord, a hockey stick and floor lamp
with shade still attached, a calendar
turning its month over at last.

Avalanche

She felt the snowfield break beneath her boots,
heard the boom as the fracture spread eight, nine
hundred yards left and right across the ridge.

She remembered to drop her poles and kick off
her skis; she even tried swimming awhile,
but started to gag and rolled herself up,
her face tight in her mittens, the roar
working to cram her mouth and nostrils full of snow,
half the mountain slamming downhill, uprooting
trees, boulders, line-shacks, turning the night
inside out, over and over again,

Until it all settled in the dark she felt
coming to a stop around her. She remembers the chapter
on Fright and Self Control, and takes tiny helpings
of air trapped in the space her mittens made.

She has no idea which way is up. It is
darker in there than in the childhood dream
where something white was always at the window.
Now, there is no window, only tons of snow
packed hard against her, front and back,
like king-sized mattresses piled high
for the storybook princess and the pea.

She must not pass out; she knows snow is porous
enough to keep her alive, but can almost feel
the ice mask forming across her face, the breath's
own handiwork of shallow sleep.

If she is to survive, she must now force saliva
between her lips. If it heads for her chin, escape
is above; if not, she may panic and die

upside down by herself,
the acceleration of nerves, the state of being
scared to death.

She lucks out. Up is up!
She tries to come out of her bend,
and feels the slightest give along the curve
of her body. It could be an air space. There are
such things—some the size of root cellars: hard
slabs of snow tumbled together like a house of cards.

She turns and finds she can move her head; leaning,
digging with her elbow, she drops off
to the left, like falling out of bed.

She stands on a slanting floor in the blackest dark
she has ever been in. She begins
feeling her way around her cell, and something
flaps across her face. She grabs at it
and holds on, hoping it is still intact. It
is the avalanche cord, orange and long, that unfurled
from its cannister on impact
when she belly-flopped at the top of the mountain.
She is hooked to it and has to believe the other end
is where it belongs: waving merrily above her grave.

They will find her soon, she is sure, headlamps flicking
across the terrain; they will tug at her cord,
signalling as they probe and dig. She continues along
the wall, getting the contour of the place.
There are alleyways everywhere, but they may be
dead ends; besides, she wants her cord
to have all the slack it needs.

On the nearest block, she finds a tilted shelf
of torn ice, beneath it: a frond of hemlock; she eases it

out, hoping it is still attached, but it comes off
in her hand. She sets it aside and becomes aware
of the fragrance filling the room.

She squats and closes her eyes, as if
she were in the forest after a good downhill run,
and thinks: Perhaps she can tunnel to a tree;
perhaps there will be a door there, hinged
by elves. "Grendel" she says aloud. "Mab, Lizard
Leg, Horse-Nettle."

But she has missed the password; nothing opens
anywhere. She laughs at herself and shakes her head.
What to do. Her rucksack is gone, ripped off
up top. She could use something to eat.
She has pockets everywhere, zippers, buttons, snaps,
but she comes up empty,
except for car keys and a penlight
dead on its chain.

She knows there is air for a day or more,
and remembers the boy in Norway buried for a week.
She wants to eat snow but doesn't want cramps.
She wants to dig but thinks of cave-ins.
She needs to scream but no one will hear.

It's high in her chest, something
like the ache from running too hard too long
before you run through it and out
the other side. She lets it come on.

It's as though she's been scolded and sent
to her room. She takes off her mittens and goes
to her knees to fill each with snow. "Bad girl"
she says and hurls her mittens away, starting to sob
only a little, mumbling frightened things.

And then the right foot. She stands
and stomps the snow, running her fingers up
the avalanche cord, still safe in the air
where it hangs. "Mustn't pull. Good girl. Mustn't
pull." And she starts
reeling it in, an inch at a time, allowing
the orange ribbon to slip through the roof
like a thread from her mother's hem,
curling at her feet, the last of it fluttering
across her face and down her arms.

She sits and finds the end of the cord. She puts it
to her thumb and starts rolling it up, 'round and 'round,
neat as a pin it goes, a giant thimble growing
in the dark. But she tires of her game and crawls away
in a widening circle in search of the hemlock branch.
She buries her face in it and strips a handful
of needles, rubbing them between her palms, inhaling
the sweet sticky smear she has made of herself.

She plants the rest of the branch upright
in the floor, and lies down to face it, patting
the snow, telling it things, crossing
and uncrossing her legs behind her.

She saw him arrive in a jumble of fire, a wee
bit of a thing on the lowest limb. He wore
a green jerkin with hollow stone buttons and knickers
puffed to the bands. She started to hum
to see if he'd dance in his circle of light,
and the jig that he did made her laugh in a giggle
inside. She watched him kick at the base of the tree
and bark fall away from the door.

With his hat held aloft and a sweep of his arm,
he bade her Good Day and Come In. It was in half light

she climbed, hand over hand, the elf
urging her on from behind; up, up
to the uppermost rung
to a four-legged chair and a window of sticks
tied together with vines, and a view
of the snowfield below.

They were there, starting the scuffline by moonlight,
wands marking the turn where the ski pole appeared.
She is tired from climbing and wants to sleep;
she will call to them later, after they find
whatever it is they lost.

Laid Off

The woman behind the loan desk says No
for the last time and waits for him to leave.
He stands and makes sure his sleeve
brushes against a stack of file folders,
leaving a clutter of paper at her feet;
he doesn't look back.

Out on the steps, he hears the guard
locking the doors behind him. Three o'clock.
He buttons the only button left on his coat
and straightens the paperclip he took
when her back was turned. He sticks it
in his collar, feeding it
through the flap on the other side,
twisting it back on itself,
against the wind, before heading north
along the tracks.

The rain has turned to sleet, and he looks
for a stopping place. A tavern roof rises close
to the roadbed, but he knows
he's not welcome there.

He takes the wad of deposit slips he stole
from the glass bin and lets it fly,
dozens of giant flakes
coming back in his face, a few settling off
to his left, dark down the sloping gravel
where the stagnant water waits.

He's soaking through but can almost see
the tunnel beneath the interstate; if no one
is there, he can get a few minutes rest.

It's no place to stay too long; beatings
are as common as dogs.

He tries taking two ties at a time,
but settles for a shorter stride, squinting
his way to the underpass.

The walls are wet from seepage, but he's safe
from sleet. He squats on the foot-ledge
and pulls his arms close to his chest, blowing
into one fist and then the other, his cheeks
puffed and blotched, his toes working themselves
like fingers in wet mittens, the girders
rumbling overhead under the weight
of holiday traffic leaving the city.
He's tempted to stay the night

But hears them in time to make a run for it,
three toughs heading home for supper, shouting
him out, swearing to take his shoes
the next time they catch him napping.

He stops beyond the bend and sits down
on the track, the same roadbed, the same
water, blacker in the dusk. He hears
the train downtrack, the engine light closing in.

He decides to get out of the way in time
to watch the commuters
dry behind glass. He feels for the largest stone
he can find, and holds it lightly, ready
to shatter a window, but lets it fall
down the ravine, the caboose trailing
its red lantern, pitching him back into darkness.

He sits on the rail trembling
beneath him, the sleet becoming snow. He curls

out his tongue, allowing flake
after flake to land and dissolve; others stay
whole on his eyelids, closed against the sky.

He wishes he had gloves
and a pair of buckle boots—the ones
he had when he was growing up, when
his mother would turn them half inside out
to warm over the register.

He can feel the flannel lining, the gloves
supple and light on his hands,
the new smell of leather
that means everything.

Breaking the Seal

He obeys his holy orders
and parks at the convent wall,
taking the path on the public side
of the fence. Once inside,

He heads through the trees
to the chapel doors, where he uses the key
that weighs heavy in his pocket all week long.

He enters the confessional and waits
for them to come: novices
half his age, lastingly wed
to their vows they seem
anxious to pass their mild offenses
through his forgiving hands, and to do
what he says they must.

He admits to having thoughts, but keeps them
under control; he enjoys
their supplication, rehearses what it is
he says to them, but wonders
if they ever wish they knew
the man behind the cloth.

He receives them each in turn,
the youngest always last, innocent
to a fault. He hears her leave in prayer,
the residue of her voice filtered
by the screen, the clean breath,
the slightest touch of starch adrift
in the dark
his fingers long to explore.

Safe Distance

(SD=300 x cube root of pounds explosive)

At seven thousand feet, the underpinnings of clouds
look more like wind-ice on a mountain lake,
its mist working among the curls, the sun
slanting its shadows toward Canada, as his last day
on Earth opens its wings.

His leather envelope made it through the gate
with him; he holds it flat to his chest
as the 727 banks hard to the left, avoiding those
who hurt him most; he leans back, aware
of the headrest crinkling behind him; he wonders
whether the night crew changed the paper
or if he's deep in dandruff or Vitalis
or the female breath of hair rinse
ready to fill his nostrils if he turns; perhaps
a long blonde hair has already settled
in his own; he keeps his hands to himself & sees
the No Smoking sign still aglow; he smiles,
remembering his room

On West Seneca, the essentials laid out on the bed
last night: upholstery thread tight on its spool,
the plastic spoon he licked clean yesterday
afternoon, two baggies of black powder, the socks
they are flying in, & the ampule of mercuric
fulminate that will blow them apart, but now waits
cool in its cotton mesh, safe in a Parker pen
whose sac of blue ink lies unplugged & limp
in a dresser drawer he will never open again.

His hands are on his lap, a scar
on one knuckle where a hacksaw jumped his grip

in his father's shop; it fades when he stretches it;
he makes it disappear again before tasting
the moisture forming on his palms: almost warm
enough to detonate the ampule riding in his vest;
he tries to recall the doubting Thomas who left
a hand in Bomb School, but comes up with only half
a name; he folds his fingers into fists
& is bemused, thinking of them gone astray.

He will distribute them soon, the brochures,
simple in design: xeroxed back-to-back after
hours, folded once, black letters on yellow stock,
elite type, precise language; they will read
how he learned as a boy in a cellar
that chemicals do what they say they do;
they will see the formula & wish themselves down
behind trees or hillside where they might
burrow & climb for their lives.

By paragraph twelve he'll be holding the pilots
at bay, having them squat at the cockpit walls,
trying to find more distance from the ampule
they watch slide from its pen to be lashed
to the curve of the spoon, thread holding it open
& bare for the heat his fingers & thumb
are frantic to give.

He wonders if some hero will make his move
& fail; the priest will mention Hellfire, a parent
her child, a son his mother dying in Sunnyside;
some will say nothing at all as they read
how the spoon will be laced to the baggies & stuffed
overhead in the console
to melt all controls to their pinnings
when the ampule goes wild at his touch.

The cabin sign is off;
a stewardess is hustling drinks in First Class;
he unbuckles himself & stands,
adjusting the black powder socks that dangle
from his belt; he unzips the envelope & removes
the brochures; the stern man across the aisle
accepts one & flicks on the overhead light;
it is 8:13; they are due at La Guardia at nine.

THREE

Before Thee I Stand

Going the Distance

The late June sun had come in the window
over his mother's bed, and he used it
to make shadows on the wall, but they came out
looking like ropes, tight twisted things,
wrapped around themselves. He flicked
all ten fingers and closed them
into fists, pressing knuckles to knuckles
until they hurt, as they did
when he'd fight in the schoolyard.

They were big hands, like Grandfather Fitz's
he'd been told, the man long dead, whose sepia eyes
never closed as they stared him down
from the opposite corner, the oval portrait
leaning too close on its wire.

He knew he shouldn't look below the frame
at his sleeping mother, but he did,
sometimes, and saw things. He did not
enjoy seeing her nightgown hiked up
to her hips when the sheet slipped away
in the night. He wished he could yank it
down, tuck it in, pin it tight
to the binding running around the mattress.

What he liked best was lying at first light,
her long braid brown and inviting,
almost touching the floor. But he grew
afraid when once she half-roused
and turned, a shoulder strap slack enough
to reveal a breast, the only one
he'd ever seen. He tried to remember
nursing at it, wondering if he'd fondled

the braid as he fed, if she caressed
him in his nakedness.

But then he'd shut his eyes and turned
to the wall, getting his face
as close to it as he could, his left hand
strained and flat against the cool blue plaster.
Often, near morning, she would say things
in dream, and he would cover his ears and hum
until he heard nothing at all.

And now, on this the last day
he'd ever have to spend in grammar school,
he lay awake in the room he'd always shared
with her, and thought about

His father far down the hall
in his chamber, his bothersome snoring
muffled from Mother's delicate sleep;
his sister close on the other side
of the wall, in the room he wanted
for himself. He shut off the alarm

Before it clanged and was relieved to find
his mother wrapped, tangled,
only a big toe jutting out for air
in the narrow space between them.

Downstairs, he smeared a piece of bread
with apple butter and sat on the porch,
remembering the summer morning his sister
forced him to stay on the bottom step
while she repeated the lie of a woman
in a long black car who would soon be at the curb;
she would wear a black dress and gloves
and laced boots. She would take him away.

He licked the last of the apple butter
from his thumb and went off the back way,
over the fence and down the path;
he was late and stopped to get
a scolding note from Sister Helena.

When the last of all bells rang for the day,
he opened his locker and stuck
his copy of Ring magazine in his back pocket
and took the leftover bottle
of ink to smash against the brick wall
rising high over the rectory window, someone
yelling, promising there'd be hell to pay,
calling him by name but in a voice that knew
it was best to leave him alone.

At the end of the block,
he settled under a tree, the largest maple
on the Town Hall lawn; he thought
of it as his own and came to it
on such days. He pulled
his magazine out and uncurled it, Billy Conn
on the cover, his cut-man taking the stool
out of the corner, the ropes tight behind him,
thick and twisted, wrapped in tape.

The idea hit him like a quick jab:
he could have a ring! The hardware store
had clothesline. He slipped one inside his jacket
and paid for the other two. And then home.

No one was there, and he went to the cellar.
He undid the clotheslines and looped
the three ends around the first steel pole
that supported the main beams of the house.

And then the braiding: crossing the strands,
as he'd seen his mother do a thousand times
at her vanity, stopping
to straighten the snarls, to tighten
the loops; inch by inch it grew
from pole to pole: the top rope
of his own ring, his own place,
the rope burns on his hands
reminding him of the shadows on their wall
this morning, Grandfather's eyes,
his mother's long plaited hair
half undone by sleep.

He wouldn't use tape; he wanted the strands
as they were. The last knot tied, he slapped
the rope and it almost sang back.
He went to a neutral corner and saw Billy Conn
coming at him. He circled to his left
and kept away till the round was over.

He stepped out of the ring and did
some shadowboxing near the washtubs,
banging away at the air, talking himself
into a frenzy, taking a few shots to the head,
the gut, moving away, jabbing, sticking,
until he was soaking wet.

The faucet squeaked when he turned it
on full force, cold water drowning out
everything, hands splashing it everywhere,
his shirt and slacks and undershorts
peeled off, a bath towel stiff but dry
hanging from its nail near the stairs.

Barefoot and naked,
he stepped back under the rope

to dry off in the ring, wrapping the towel
tight at the waist, tucking it in,
arms held overhead in victory.

And then the army cot, folded
within reach, to be snapped open
and snugged up against the pole
closest to the furnace, two full floors
beneath Mother's bed.

He stretched out on the taut canvas,
his left arm across his face,
the right finding the braided rope,
curling his fingers around it,
tightening his grip, running it slowly
out and back as far as he could, his mouth
going dry as he felt the strands rise
and disappear in the palm of his hand.

FOUR

Behold the Handmaid

Fitz and the Gandy Dancers

*(The railroad track-laborer often appeared to be dancing as he'd
swing and heave the tools of his trade, manufactured somewhat
exclusively in Chicago by the now defunct Gandy Corporation.)*

His visits home are risings from the dead:
the walk down Woodward from the depot,
Kittie waiting at the doorstep, smoothing
the clean white apron she starched
and ironed an hour ago.

There's always the unwinding, the hiding away
of the suitcase as though he were going
to stay, the toothbrush back in its circle
at the sink, the hairbrush upside down
on the shelf, the drapes thrown open
in the far bedroom, closed off when he's gone.

No matter the season, Fitz goes by himself
alongside the barn to the stream he compares
to a mile of track west of Galeton, the same
dips and turns. He prefers the stream,

But his crew's not there clearing the way
for the 9:53 from Buffalo, waving it on
before heading out to fix whatever
it rattled loose
between milepost #599 and #607.

There'll be joints in need of shims,
a dozen or more spikes riding up, a tie
edging away from its stones; everything
scrawled on a pad
they hand him at quitting time.

The stream is almost quiet. The rime
that flared the willow is gone, the beards
of ice thinning along the crags, one more winter
giving up to thaw; it's good

To be away from the gangshack awhile.
He spends too much time in it
staring through window dust, thinking
of his men, downtrack, taking a break,
their tin cups in the canvas sack
lashed to the handcar, the gallon of coffee
tied thick with newspapers. He'd be with them
if he could, but there's no going back
from foreman to gandy.

Sunday night he'll be back at The Inn
sharing another meal with boarders
he'd rather see passing on a train,
and then the hours alone
thinking letters he will never write:

To Lyle at dental school to ease up
on his work. To Kell at U.B. to lay off
the parties. And Kathleen
spending the last year of high school
in an empty house with her mother.

A small shelf of ice gives way
at his feet. He watches it turn in place
and head downstream.

The night has come cold. He looks back
toward the house and imagines Kittie
calling him to bed, the patch of ice
lost in the current some thirty ties away.

Sunday Dinner

Linen napkins, spotless from the wash, starched
and ironed, smelling like altar cloths. Olives
and radishes wet in cut glass, a steaming gravy bowl
attached to its platter, an iridescent pitcher cold
with milk, the cream stirred in moments before.

The serving fork, black bone at the handle, capped
in steel, tines sharp as hatpins. Stuffed celery,
cut in bite-sized bits, tomato juice flecked
with pepper, the vinegar cruet full to the stopper
catching light from the chandelier.

Once-a-week corduroyed plates with yellow trim,
a huge mound of potatoes mashed and swirled.
Buttered corn, side salads topped with sliced tomatoes,
a tall stack of bread, a quarter pound of butter
warmed by its side. And chicken, falling off the bone:
crisp skin baked sweet with ten-minute bastings.

Homemade pies, chocolate mints and puddings,
coffee and graceful glasses of water, chipped ice
clinking the rims.

Cashews in a silver scoop, the centerpiece a milkglass
compote with caved-in sides, laced and hung
with grapes, apples, and oranges for the taking.

The Woman in the Corner House

doesn't complain anymore
about her husband's late nights or drinking
or, most especially, the way he left
his pajamas on the bathroom floor
when he'd come downstairs, freshly shaved
and showered, ready for his day
at the office where he died.

She used to wave goodbye through the oval
front door, and trudge upstairs
to see if he'd remembered. She'd pick them up,
wishing he were still in them, shaking
them out, scolding him
in a voice no more than a whisper.

She'd fold them and tuck them
under his pillow in the big double bed
they'd shared for thirty years in the room
over the parlor and its piano.

She'd buy new ones once a year,
grumbling about him
right there in the men's department,
deciding on a style that seemed young, never
grey, usually without buttons, and always
summer-weight and tall.

The pair she bought last Thursday had blue
stripes. She had them gift-wrapped
in the store's silver foil and took them
home where she left them
on the edge of the bed he'd slept in
for the last time a month ago.

After the local news and weather,
she locked the cellar door and left
the pantry bulb ablaze,
to keep the shadows in their place,
and went upstairs.

The bedside lamp shed light
on the box, waiting in its trim.
She opened it and took the pajamas
to her lap: the noisy sheet of tissue lost
within the folds; sixteen more pins
to add to the scrap of flannel she kept
tacked above the sewing machine.

She was pleased to find the inspection slips.
Number four had checked the bottoms; number
twelve had seen to the tops.

He would have liked them. No buttons, bordered
cuffs, four snaps on the fly, and enough room
in the seat to turn over
and over in his sleep.

His pillow was where it belonged.
She laid the pajamas full length along his side
of the bed, the left leg bent at the knee,
where she could feel it on her back, if he were there.

Come morning, she will drop them
on the bathroom floor on her way downstairs.

The neighbor children won't notice her
waving from the door, but when the school bus leaves,
she will close the curtains and go back
upstairs to find
what she knows she will find, and take them
in her arms.

A Visit Home

The bottom sweater button
is in the next to bottom hole,
and his mother's fingers almost
find it out, but climb instead
to the polished head of a brooch:
a maiden blushing to the left, hair
falling across a shoulder
bared in sunlight.

Something about the eyes tells her
she should know him, perhaps
the young man who brings her groceries
or Father Sullivan
dressed for a day off.

But no. The voice is more comfortable
than that; it fits the neighborhood.
His hair is going grey; tanned,
he must spend time along the lake.
The eyes react
as her father's would: cut glass
catching light

Shed by a flowered bulb in the ceiling
where they stand stopped
in the upstairs hall, she
at her bedroom door; her married son
nearer the guest room, a step away,
dressed from the shower
hardly used since he lived at home.

She'd like to have a towel
from the linen closet, one of the long

fluffy ones they used to save for company,
and wrap it 'round his head, the way
his mother must have done
before he grew so tall.

He seems familiar,
but she can't believe the name
he used for her.

She takes his arm
and turns his face up
toward the light, as mothers do,
and finally asks the question:
Whose boy are you?

Beneath a Mansard Roof

She wakens to an attic room
whose curtains have gone limp with rain.
The rosary beads that helped her turn
to sleep still lie half-said
across her flannel gown.

If she could lift her head
enough to see beyond the sill, she'd know,
she thinks, what place she's in.
Which means, perhaps, she's not at home,
for if she is where is the sash
she pulls on when she needs to sit
for meals or evening prayers?

And what about the ceiling?
Those squares are nothing like they are
at home. Although she can't recall
quite what they ought to be, she knows
these aren't the same. Why, what if
they begin to fall? What if
she counts them, row by row, and has
an extra number when she's through?
Why would anyone paste a ceiling up
like that? Where are the nails?

It must be winter still. She'll ask
for another blanket when they bring her
toast and tea. Up on an elbow,
her woolen robe just out of reach, she sees
the maple start its contradiction:
its closest branch full-leaf and bowing
against the window screen.

Back deep in her pillow, she decides
to close her eyes to see if she can figure
out how long and who and when and where,
but drifts away instead to watch the specks
dart beneath her lids. She moves her eyes
from side to side and finds a summer sky,
and sleeps beneath it.

Feeding the Birds

She doesn't hear her lunch arrive, but is shaken
awake to drink her medication and to be cranked
upright for the tray; she bibs her napkin
and takes a spoon to her tea in near silence.

She's hoped for purple finches and gets them,
two by two at the window ledge, poking
around in the spillage of thistle and millet,
cracked corn and shucks of sunflower seeds.

Then up to the feeder they go, held somehow
to the glass, and she watches them holding on
in midair, the others waiting in hemlocks
on the far side of the wall.

One finch looks in on her,
tilts its dull raspberry head and is gone,
its mate intent on the meal, a bold
pale eyebrow underscoring the crown.

She would like to see their nest:
a scoop of grass and twigs, usually lined
with hair, often her own, back when
she'd yank the barn rope, rocking the rain barrel
on its swivel, drenching herself
in the afternoon sun, toweling and combing,
brushing and drying
on the wide flat lawn.

There were hemlocks then, and willows
along the brook, where the birds fed themselves,
as they are doing now, newcomers,

only an arm's length from her bed,
where she strains in a harness of cloth
to see them landing on the sill.

FIVE

World without End

Those Who Trespass

He'd find them among fallen limbs and brush
in the pitiful stretch of trees
they call their woods: stones the size
of grapefruits, lugged out to the driveway
to be washed off with the garden hose
and left to bake on the blacktop
in the high sun before being tucked away
in the trunk of the car, along the sides,
some down in the well, snug against the spare
held fast by the stretch-strap doubling
as the tire-iron brace, a four-pronged plus sign
looking more like a silver cross the way
it is propped, as though its Christ had fallen
off, perhaps still there laid out
among the stones.

Headed for Buffalo, the outskirts,
the homestead where there were no rocks
to line the rose garden, houses no more
than a car's width away from the next,
the narrow concrete tilting
toward Bannigan's front porch.

And his parents would be there, pacing
the sunporch, waiting for the visit to begin:
five days of clutter and talk, sleeping bags
and diapers, suitcases, books,
hanging clothes, shopping bags; space enough
in the guest room.

And then the stones, last, always
last: a few at a time; each placed
ceremoniously along the rim of the rose garden

that curled against the side of the garage
to the back picket fence, turning left
at the Broderson's shed and back
toward the house.

Father is dead; Mother is gone, and soon
strangers will be moving in. But the stones
are still there, years of stones. Last night
he went off alone to do something about that.
He took only the three-inch paintbrush saved
from his father's workbench, one
of a dozen washed after every use, never
to be thrown away, clean in its plastic pouch,
the snap still intact.

Seven hours by train, a short walk
to the Delaware bus, twenty minutes to the city
line. He gets off a stop early and crosses
the street to the hardware store; the name
has changed, common as a tenpenny nail.

He chooses a gallon of black enamel
and feels the plank floor shudder
beneath him as the vibrator-stand
shakes the can to a blur on the counter.

> *His mother's hands are shaking in her room, some*
> *400 miles downstate; if she had lids on the cups*
> *she would spill less tea on her sweaters and robe.*
> *He may suggest it to the home.*

> *Now, at 10:30 in the morning, she is saying*
> *her first rosary of the day, the floor nurse leading*
> *her on, bead by bead, as the paint slaps against its lid*
> *only a block away from the altar rail*
> *where she knelt for half a lifetime.*

She doesn't know
what she is doing; she is seventeen again:
Springville, her brothers bringing her candies, Papa
home on weekends from the railroad gang,
her mother, rosary in hand at bedtime, and Kathleen
sleeping with her own beads under her pillow,
the same rosary she holds in her grape-veined hands
this morning, a day's journey from where he stands
waiting for his twenty-dollar bill to be broken.

She is alone for the first time in weeks:
the nurse has left to check on a noise in the hall,
and Mother goes on inventing melodies and words
to replace the orthodox prayers once her own.
In her wheelchair, the canvas waistband tight
as a saint's hairshirt, she feels
the beads loose in her hand. She fingers them,
their roundness, small as pebbles, smaller
than the stones her son has gone to see again.

She is drawn to the beads, sensing nourishment.
Her lips are moving in prayers
never heard before; her tongue is extended, her eyes
closed. She bends closer to the beads, accepting
them now like the host safe in her mouth, sliding
slowly as forgiveness on the same saliva
the aides dab away with tissues.

But now, it serves her well: for the beads
have slipped fully beyond the lips; they could
be green peas all in a row tumbling from a spoon,
beginning their descent. No pain. No outcry;
she is deep in a tangled meditation; only
the crucifix is left dangling against her chin,
its small silver link holding fast to the first
of its fifty-nine beads.

63

Christ is in His diaper and the thorns are intact;
He is swaying slightly swaying, His features
rubbed away by Mother's mothering. They retrieve
the rosary and dry it well enough
for her to go on to the next decade, the connected beads
back where they belong: in the tiny palm
that waited like a cradle or a font
or a crypt dark behind a large washed stone.

The paint can is freed from its shaking. He takes
the gallon as it is, swinging on its wire handle,
and drops the change in his side pocket.

The town seems almost the same: the village hall,
the playground at the corner, Kay's Drugstore
bought out and revamped from counter
to name. The sun is hot as he turns down Lincoln
Boulevard. The house is vacant; he decides
not to use the spare key for any last look.

The backyard is his grotto and he goes to it.
The stones are still in their looped line
skirting the edge of the rose garden. He stands
frozen in place. He wants all of the stones;
he wants to take them back to the ground he walks
every evening, the frail run of trees
that flanks his house.

He feels for his rosary and finds it
in his suitcoat pocket, kept there for good luck.
He takes out the beads on barstools sometimes,
to fondle them in the dim light, saying
their prayers half in a trance, and in churches
he needs to find when he is alone on the road,
cities he doesn't want to see ever again.

The stones must stay. And so he begins:
within minutes they are laid out
in a wide circle. Some of them tipping, a few
already out of ranks, but each assigned a plot
of ground: the paternosters, the aves,
the tenth aves each doubling as a Gloria Patri.

The shrubbery encircling the yard is thick
enough to hide him from the neighbors. He stands
at the back of the lawn, at the strand of beadstones
which must stray from the others so that he
might affix the crucifix-stone to its tip.
He knew back home which stone it must be:
the one with the purple vein running around
its middle, and it is there.

He loosens the lid of the gallon
with the half dollar he brought from his dresser
drawer, the chifforobe which once stood
in his father's room and now holds his own socks
and shirts and bonds and bills. The paint
is rich, the brush still soft; he can smell
the turpentine on the bristles, dry and stained
deep with many colors far down in the base,
each a different Saturday morning project done
with his father on this property, before the stones,
before almost anything.

He kneels at the first stone and grabs too quickly,
anxious to see the purple run of color, and jams
his thumb, blood forming already beneath the nail.
He replaces the stone and paints a rough cross
on it, trying to leave the vein purple
as a cinch for the stipe. He takes a giant step
to where the next stone lies: the paint

goes on with hardly a trace of dirt; another
step and he is past The Lord's Prayer, onto the first
trio of aves: the Hail Marys, one like the next.
The black is as lush as the counterman
said it would be.

Another single bead, and he finds himself
praying aloud, loud enough only for a stone
to hear. Another space and then on to the flat slab
of sandstone he knew he would use
to connect the circle of decades. He gives it
two brush strokes, unbroken,
a child's attempt at the ancient fish, good enough
for anyone who knows.

Three spaces beyond the fish lies a speckled stone;
it goes black, flush to the grass. Nine more
go quickly, slopping the paint in a blob
on top, all at once, scampering back
and forth to smooth out the drippage, ripping away
the blades of grass
that are stained, stuffing them in his back pockets.
He says the prayers as he paints his way
through the next ten; one has a bit of moss
from the shaded area along the spilloff spout
on the garage roof, the others bare
as the edge of grave markers.

It takes three Hail Marys to paint
a hail mary, the phrase "blessed art thou among women"
the line that slows him down: he finds himself
repeating it, remembering the pitchers
of lemonade Mother would leave in the shade
with chipped ice and a tall glass when he
would use the handmower on a hot day.

He is rubbing the grass now, the way
he did when he was a boy, after cutting it twice,
once fence to drive and, again, from garden
to house. He would sit and sip from the sweating glass;
the grass, the smell, the silent creatures
he'd disturbed, all
holier and cleaner than the wood trimming
the stations of the cross in the church a block away
over the back fence. He runs his hand
across the grass until it hits his leg
and wakes him to his task.

Decade two. The stones are dusty and pitted.
It all takes too long and he wonders
if the weather will hold. He crawls on
to The Lord's Prayer, three spaces away; he smiles
as he comes to the words, "Those who trespass,"
and looks over his shoulder toward a space
in the hedge, but knows that
what he is doing is his to do.

The third and fourth are almost too much.
The paint needs stirring, the brush is filled
with dirt; his time is running out. If
he were to show anyone a decade, it would not be
either of these. The paint is too thick, the grass
too black, the stone-face showing through too often.

He must finish and get away; he feels it
in his wrists and ankles. He wonders if he should
have come at all. His thumb,
with its nail blood dried black, is numbing.
He needs to be home, close to his own
ring of stones at the far end of the property
where he can sit and poke at the mild fires

he builds there, feeding the flames
with twigs and branches fallen on their own,
the rocks large enough not to split from the heat,
high enough to contain the blaze.

But it is time for his best work.
The paint goes on like cream, as thick
as the cream that came
in the bulb-topped bottles of the forties
that the milkman would leave in the back hall
during the war if they'd remember to prop
the shirtcard cow in the window alongside
the sign for the iceman and breadman,

Smooth as the blade of grass he holds still
between his lips, thin and slick, not a blade
to crush between thumbs
to make an unseemly noise, not one that would grow
in a back lot, but one like all the others
in this yard, planted by Father, tended
by Father, watered by Father at dusk while other lawns
went to seed and crabgrass and weed no one
could name. It tastes good and clean and cool.

And now it is done. The last beadrock black
as the pieces of coal he was allowed to pitch
into the yawning furnace,
when Father would bank the fire,
at nine-thirty every night, so that they could awaken
in Lake Erie winters to heat
rising from the floor grids.

He looks back at the house, up
at the window where the afternoon light
is spreading its daily shadow across the corner

of the small blue room he'd shared
with his mother.

He goes to his knees and puts the lid back
on the empty can. He wipes the brush across the label,
the brand name, the directions, the cautions,
cleaning the bristles as best he can. He will
finish the job as his father would have him do,
but not here; back home, at his own bench
in his own garage, where he belongs.

He slips the brush into its plastic sleeve
and drops it carefully into his inside suitcoat
pocket and walks to the corner of the house
where the same garbage cans wait hidden
behind the spruce trees. He lowers the container
far down inside the first and heads for the street;
he does not look back.

He has his wallet, his ticket home,
his father's brush. He is listening to the angelus
tolling from the parish belfry: six o'clock.
But there is something else, quieter than the bells
calling the villagers to prayer, something
closer. It is his mother's voice, restored,
the same voice that used to call to him
from the kitchen window; she is obeying the ringing
of the bells; she is intoning the beads
he has left in her name beneath the Niagara sky:
the threat of rain diminished, a healing breeze
from the distant river
drying the rocks where they lie.